SMOKESCREEN

a collection of writing by pupils, parents and staff
from Sandwell Schools

compiled and edited by **Dave Reeves**

illustrations by **Adele Stach-Kevitz**

Copyright © 1999

THIS BOOK CONTAINS A PERSONAL HEALTH WARNING

Published by
The Moving Finger
PO Box 2923, SMETHWICK,
West Midlands. B67 5AG

for **Sandwell Health Authority** in partnership with
Sandwell Education Department.

SANDWELL
Health
Action Zone
Working in Partnership

ISBN 1 871296 81 1

Design:
Sakab Bashir

Illustrations:
Adele Stach-Kevitz p.13, 18, 26, 29, 42, 50 ,53, 59
or by the pupils themselves.

FOREWORD

Sandwell Health Authority in partnership
Making it matter in schools and the wider community, with
Opportunities for pupils, parents and governors to work together,
Keeping health a central issue.
Employing a resident writer Dave Reeves
Sandwell Education Authority organised
Creative Writing Workshops
Raising awareness, and in a project
Embracing both the young and the old,
Educating the community on smoking cessation.
Nothing is more powerful than the written word.

Sue Trotman
Sandwell Education Authority Advisory Consultant

THANKS TO

Margaret Storrie - Sandwell Education Authority Adviser
Chris Saxon - Sandwell Health Authority
Smoking Prevention Co-ordinator
Gill Cole - Schools Administration

The pupils, staff and parents of:

Abbey Junior
Arden School
Bleakhouse Junior
Great Bridge Primary
Hollyhedge Primary
Langley Primary
Mesty Croft Primary
Old Park Primary
Rowley Hall Primary
Sacred Heart RC Primary
Shireland Language College
St Huberts RC Primary
St John Bosco RC Primary
St Margaret's CE Primary
St Mary's RC Primary
St Mary Magdalene CE Primary
Tividale Hall Primary
Wodensborough Community Technical College

and all of the schools who participated in this project.

CONTENTS

CONTENTS cont.

INTRODUCTION

So much creativity is used in the promotion of tobacco that it was good to give people the opportunity to use their own imaginations to look at the issues and the images portrayed.

Late in 1998 and early in 1999 I worked with pupils, parents and staff in schools throughout Sandwell exploring the theme of smoking. A project which at first sight might have appeared limited in its scope never once became a drag. In what turned out to be a thoroughly inspiring residency we investigated the hazards of tobacco smoking and the long term effects it has on our lives. Cigarettes were personified as invading armies and dragons bespoiling the landscape of the body; they were compared to bombs, daggers, tanks and missiles - weapons all. They became volcanoes molten with destruction and the nicotine stained, King of Smo (the Smo-King) taxed his subjects mercilessly. There was an excitement in the use of language which produced some truly memorable images and poems.

Much more writing was produced than it was possible to fit into this book so I'd like to take this opportunity to thank all those who took part for their hard work. Sessions inspired and informed each other, passing ideas around the borough. In that sense this book is the work of all of those who participated, not just those whose individual poems feature in its pages.

I hope that you enjoy the writings, that they amuse you and make you see things slightly differently. If just one image remains with you and makes you think again about the whole business of smoking we will have been successful getting our message across, but I hope a lot more of the work stays in your memory, as it has in mine.

Dave Reeves - writer & editor

MY ADVICE

Why do people want to smoke,
When all it does is make them choke?
Don't they realise what harm it does
To themselves and the rest of us?

It is well known that smoking can kill,
Or, at least, can make you very ill.
My advice would be never to start,
Look after your lungs and your heart.

Luke Bodman

WHAT GOOD IS A FAG?

My cigarette is a pair of socks
Plaguing and stinking out the house.

My cigarette is a horoscope
Telling me when I'm going to die.

What good is a fag?

My cigarette is a dart
Aiming for the bulls eye of my heart.

What good is a fag?

My cigarette is a compulsive liar
Saying "I am good for you".

My cigarette is a windmill
Slowly grinding my life away.

What good is a fag?

My cigarette is a bully
Hurting me, and hurting me, and hurting me.

What good is your fag?

Brogan Darby

WAR CRY

Cigarettes are an army
The warriors are robbing your money
The warriors have knives, cutting through your
heart
The warriers have a war cry:
    COUGH, COUGH, COUGH!

Cigarettes are an army
The warriors have shields to stop your circulation
The warriors pierce your heart with swords
The warriors shoot bombs through your lungs
The warriors have a war cry:
    COUGH, COUGH, COUGH!

**Adam Craig, Samuel Stirrup, Luke Murphy,
Luke Barnsley & Rhys Maher**

ONE-WAY ROAD

You think that you're as smart as Einstein
but did Einstein ever smoke?
You think you're one of the smart crowd
but your clothes smell.
You think you're so hard
but really you're a nervous wreck.
You think you're one of the pop stars
but your fingers are yellow.
You think you're hugging a teddy
but you have a plastic bag over your head.
You think you're card Smiley
but your teeth are nasty and yellow.
You think you're on the road to fame
but you're on the one-way road to death.

Alison Dunn

BIT BY BIT

A cigarette is a doorway to death
opening at every puff
destroying you
bit by bit, slowly, slowly.

A cigarette is a bomb
blowing the colour out of your lungs
destroying you
bit by bit, puff by puff.

A cigarette is poison ivy
creeping slowly, ending your life gradually
bit by bit, slowly, slowly.

Luke Brookes

WITHOUT YOU

Without you, I would have a better life
Without you, I would have far less strife
Without you, my children would not fear
Without you, more people would be here
Without you, I would not be writing a will
Without you, play and leisure would not kill

Samantha Warwick

IT'S NOT A JOKE

Your friends ask you
Do you want a drag?
Think about your health
Let them keep their fag.

Your friends tell you
It's cool to smoke
Think about your health
Smoking is not a joke.

Mahsood Hussain

SAVE YOURSELF!

A cigarette is like the sun
burning away your health.
You might as well put
your cigarettes on the shelf
and save yourself.

A cigarette is a skunk
making your clothes smell.
Save yourself!

A cigarette is ink from a leaky pen
staining your fingers.
Save yourself!

A cigarette is a fire
turning your lungs black with soot.
Save yourself!

A cigarette is like the sun
burning away your health.
You might as well put
your cigarettes on the shelf
and save yourself.

Katie Poole

AS HORRID AS . . .

As horrid as . . .
    Smelly sewers
    Dog muck on your shoe
    Breathing in nicotine
As horrid as . . .
    A P.C. going wrong
    Making a mistake in maths
    Smoking in front of children
As horrid as . . .
    A jet plane crashing
    Taking drugs
    Smoking
As horrid as . . .

Ashley Myers

WHAT PRICE?

Tobacco is a natural plant
Cancer is an unnatural death

Tobacco is a legal drug
Slow suicide is illegal

Tobacco raises money through taxes
Cancer charities rely on donations

Tobacco pouches are aromatic
Ash-tray breath stinks

Tobacco is a stimulant
Yet smokers get depressed

Tobacco is expensive
What price your life?

Sandra Rex

NOT ME

Tobacco - is a plant
       - it comes from America
       - it raises revenue for the government

Tobacco - is a legal drug
       - it's addictive
       - but it depresses my appetite

Tobacco - is expensive
       - is harmful
       - but it gives me a satisfying feeling

Tobacco killed my dad, but I won't let it kill me!

Etelka Beville

DARREN THE DRAGON

Darren the dragon blows out smoke,
Darren the dragon makes you choke.
Darren the dragon takes your breath away,
Darren the dragon is there every day.
Darren the dragon stops you from running,
Darren the dragon is very cunning.
Darren the dragon looks quite friendly,
Darren the dragon is very deadly.
Darren the dragon burns you up,
Darren the dragon is very tough.

Jade Ryles & Rebecca Perry

I WISH I'D NEVER SMOKED

I'm lying in my hospital bed
Needing help just to get fed
I wish I'd never smoked
Because now all I'm going to do is choke

I've been smoking for thirty years
And I've also been drinking beers
I think it is hard to get away
From those packets of fags every day

I'm helpless, sitting in my chair
A bloke needing a fag, a bloke in despair
Now I'm going to pass away

I wish I'd never had those cigarettes every day

Chris Archer, Jagdip Johal & Jason Dawes

OH, WHAT THE HELL!

Smoking is bad,
bad for your health.
You're wasting your money
but
Oh, what the hell,
it ain't my problem
if you're gonna smell.

You think it's fun
and I think it's bad.
Most of all, I think
you're just pure mad.

Joshua Ward

DO YOU WANT A FAG?

Do you want a fag?
It will make you look cool
It'll be great for a gag
You'll be the best in school.

It's bad for your lungs
And it burns your tongue
Bad for your breath
And could cause death.

Smoking - don't do it!
You can't get through it
Once you start, you just can't stop
And if you're under age,
You'll get caught by the cops.

Laura Melough & Christine Sutton

I SMOKE AND I DON'T CARE

Without a daily dose of nicotine
It's enough to make you scream.
When you see someone with a fag
You just know you have to take a drag.

The taste in your mouth,
the feel in your fingers,
The smell it makes
Just lingers and lingers.

Teachers say it's not right.
They think I'm a fool
'cause I sneak a fag
In the toilets at school.

It's okay for them,
They don't have to wait
'till twenty past three
When you're out of the gate.

Smokers tend to say
They think that they should,
They think that they're clever
They think they look good.

But they'll wake up
One warm summer's day
With a very bad cough
That won't go away.
Why didn't I listen
When my mum would say:
"You'll get lots of wrinkles.
They'll kill you one day . . .
        DEAD!"

Dionne Walton

WHO CARES?

People think I'm ugly but I'm not
The smoking helps me to calm down and look hard.
People say a cigar is a bomb blowing ashes around
But smoking is something else.
A cigarette is a dagger, stabbing you in the heart
But it is something else too.
A cigarette is a drug which kills your family and life
but WHO CARES?
I still look pretty with a cigarette in my hand.

Amandeep Dhillon

MY CIGARETTE
IS MANY THINGS

My cigarette is the wind blowing away my health
    My cigarette is many things
My cigarette is a fire burning a hole in my lungs
    My cigarette is many things
My cigarette is the night turning my lungs black
    My cigarette is many things
My cigarette is a washing machine shrinking my lungs
    My cigarette is many things

Kayleigh Deen

SELF-INFLICTED

Don't smoke because
It could make you ill.
And if you do,
You might just find
You'll need to take a pill.

After a few more
Cigarettes,
You will get addicted.
But this awful habit
You've acquired
Is mostly self-inflicted.

You must remember
It's no joke,
When someone has to
Smell your smoke.

Giuseppe D'Amore

A BULLY IS BAD
FOR YOUR HEALTH

Smoking is like being a bully,
    it can leave you with no friends.
Smoking is like painting,
    it can change the colour of your fingers.
Smoking is like being covered in plastic,
    it can take all your breath away.
Smoking is like a dart,
    it can make a hole in your heart.
Smoking is like garlic,
    it can make your breath smell.
Smoking is like a drug,
    it can kill you.
Smoking is like a sweet,
    it can change the colour of your teeth.

Jamie Tonks

SAY NO!

A cigarette is an axe murderer -
Out to kill you.

Say No, say No.
Say Let me keep my freedom,
Say Let me keep my freedom.
Say No!

A cigarette is a cork -
It stops your circulation.

Say No, say No.
Say Let me keep my freedom,
Say Let me keep my freedom.
Say No!

A cigarette is a clock -
It ticks your life away.

Say No, say No.
Say Let me keep my freedom,
Say Let me keep my freedom.
Say No!

A cigarette is a car,
Travelling at 125 miles per hour.
Once it hits you - you're dead!

Faye Kinsella

THE SMO KING

The Smo King
has yellow hair and yellow fingers.
He wants to take charge,
to ruin you inside as well as out.
Don't panic - fight back!

Neelamdeep Birdi

THE FOUNDER?

Tobacco raises money through taxes,
but I raised the money for my grandfather's funeral.

Tobacco was discovered by Columbus,
so does that mean he is the founder of lung cancer?

Tobacco depresses the appetite,
but it stimulates work for the undertaker.

Tobacco is a legal drug,
but the cost of it is a crime.

Tobacco smells great before you smoke it,
but for your lungs it STINKS!!

Wayne Simner

LEGAL

Tobacco is an addictive
       expensive
       drug
But tobacco is legal.

Tobacco is cancer inducing
       damages your life
       contains tar
But tobacco is legal.

Tobacco is a stimulant
       contains nicotine
       killed my grand-dad
But tobacco is legal.

Tobacco is lethal
       it ruins your lungs
       it ruins your life
But tobacco is legal.

Tracey Whall

KEEPING HEALTHY -
AN ABC

We love to keep fit and healthy
Apples, apparatus in the hall, athletics
Baseball, bananas, brown bread, basketball
Climbing, cricket
Dancing, diving
Exercise
We love to keep fit and healthy
Fitness, football
Gymnastics, grapes, games
Hopping, hitting, hockey
Ice skating
Jogging, jumping
We love to keep fit and healthy
Kicking a ball, kiss chase
Lifting, long jump, laughing
Milk, mangoes, marching
Nodding, netball
Oranges, orange juice, outdoors
Pears, peaches, plums, ping-pong
We love to keep fit and healthy
Quickly
Running races
Sandwiches, swimming, singing
Throwing, trampolining, tennis
Upside down we hang
We love to keep fit and healthy
Vitamins
Weight-lifting, walking, water
X-ercise! X-peditions!
Yoghurt, yo-yos
ZZzzzzz - a good night's sleep
We love to keep fit and healthy.

Old Park Primary School
Class 1SM (Mixed Y1/2)

MY UNCLE

The puffs of smoke
When my uncle comes to see me
He smokes at the table
He smokes at tea
When my mom comes in
From the kitchen
Guess what she says
Aloud again?
Get out! Get out!
Get outside!
And stay out
Or you'll not be alive!
So he stays outside
All day and night
SMOKING!

Stacey Lowe

DEATH SENTENCE

What is a cigarette?
an exhaust pipe blowing pollution into the air.

What is a cigarette?
a steam train blowing smoke through my body.

What is a cigarette?
an ashtray in my lungs, turning them black.

What is a cigarette?
a dagger stabbing at my heart.

What is a cigarette?
a death sentence.

Sukhdip Bhambra

DON'T LET THEM
TAKE CONTROL

Chorus:	Smoking cigarettes brings an army
	They camp in your veins.
2nd chorus:	Fight them!
	Don't let them take control!!!
Chorus:	Smoking cigarettes brings an army
	They build Calvary in your brain.
2nd chorus:	Fight them!
	Don't let them take control!!!
Chorus:	Smoking cigarettes brings an army
	They plant mines in the middle of your heart.
2nd chorus:	Fight them!
	Don't let them take control!!!
Chorus:	Smoking cigarettes brings an army
	They light a fire in your lungs.
2nd chorus:	Fight them!
	Don't let them take control!!!
Chorus:	Smoking cigarettes brings an army
	You've got to fight night and day
	Or they'll take your freedom away!

Jenny Willetts; Elizabeth Walker; Leanne Barr; Maria Scaroni; Kate Bishton and Daniel Ingram

THERE'S A MAN WHO WANTS TO KILL ME

There's a man who wants to kill me
by shooting me in my heart
and stabbing me in my head,
five times each,
to make sure I'm dead.

He would cut open my arms
and put in cigarettes
Then sew up my arms
with needle and thread.

He's a serial killer and he looks like this:
Tatty clothes
Bad teeth
Bad breath
Yellow fingers

He's a man of the street
with a sneaky smile
and big, smelly feet.

Stacie Randle

SMOKING

Smoking can kill
It makes you seriously ill

Smoking can rule
But is it really cool?

Smoking is bad
And smokers go mad

The rule is don't smoke
Or you will choke

Stephanie Stokes & Sheree Fitzmaurice

DO YOU LIKE . . .?

Do you like playing football?
      Then don't smoke
Because you won't run fast
      or score a goal.

Do you like having girlfriends?
      Then don't smoke
Because your teeth will be yellow
            and you'll smell like an ashtray.

Do you like being in hospital?
      Then don't smoke
Because you'll get cancer
      and heart disease.

Lance Kilkenny

WHY DO PEOPLE SMOKE?

Why do people smoke?
Do they think it's smart?
Why do they ever have to start?
Haven't they got
Any more sense,
It should be made
A criminal offence.

It pollutes the atmosphere,
It also harms people near
And hurts all those
Whom they love dear.
So before lighting up
Think again
And save yourself
A lot of pain.

Emily Taylor

DON'T SMOKE!

Don't smoke!
Don't smoke!
It will get in your throat.

Don't smoke!
Don't smoke!
It will soon make you choke.

Don't smoke!
Don't smoke!
It will also make you broke.

Nicola Evans

WHAT IS A CIGARETTE?

What is a cigarette?
A cigarette is like an old person shrinking away.
What is a cigarette?
A cigarette is like a chocolate teapot - good for nothing.
What is a cigarette?
A cigarette is like a needle pumping poison into your body.
What is a cigarette?
A cigarette is your life turning slowly to ash.
That's what a cigarette is.

Kirandeep Uppal

FIGHT BACK!

The King of Smo has yellow teeth, stinky breath and a smokey look.
The King of Smo chokes and finds it hard to breathe and
 when he talks he has a low voice and he splutters.

The King of Smo will make you pay taxes.
The King of Smo will attack you.
The King of Smo will tell you what to do.
The King of Smo will make you pass it on till everyone you know does it.

Don't let the King of Smo turn you into a different colour.
Don't let the King of Smo make you pass it on.
Don't let the King of Smo stick pins in your heart.
Don't surrender - FIGHT BACK!

Hannah Pritchard

YOU THINK . . .

You think a cigarette is a bed of relaxation
But it's a path of destruction.
You think a cigarette is a one way road to heaven
But it's a call to heaven or to hell.
You think smoking is a provider of comfort
But it's a criminal of heart disease, cancer and death.
You think smoking makes you popular
But your clothes and breath smell.
You think you won't die until you're old
But, by smoking, you're picking up a gun and committing suicide.

Natasha Perera

I SAY, I SAY

Some people say it's fun
Some people say it's wack
Some people think it's cool
Some people think it's slack.
But what I say is this today
I would never smoke today, I say
My grandad used to smoke each day
But what I say is this today
I would never smoke today, I say
This is what I say, I say.

Sarah Clewer

SMOKE RIVER

My cigarette is a river
Drowning my life

Alex Butler & Jack Dunford

GET RID

Smoking can kill
Money is wasted on cigarettes every day
One makes you want more of them
Keep it up and it will harm you
It will cause damage to your heart
Nasty tar on your lungs
Get rid of those cigarettes!

Billy Ford, Jason Hall & Danny Golding

COUGH, COUGH, COUGH, COUGH

Chris Marsh

I was in a pub one day
Cough, cough, cough, cough
Smoking my fag away
Cough, cough, cough, cough
I began to choke
Cough, cough, cough, cough
So drank some coke
Cough, cough, cough, cough

I was in bed one day
Cough, cough, cough, cough
Smoking my fag away
Cough, cough, cough, cough
Some ash fell on my sheet
Cough, cough, cough, cough
And burnt my feet!
Cough, cough, cough, cough

I was in my garden one day
Cough, cough, cough, cough
Smoking my fag away
Cough, cough, cough, cough
I slipped on some dirt
Cough, cough, cough, cough
And burnt a hole in my shirt!
Cough, cough, cough, cough

I was in the zoo one day
Cough, cough, cough, cough
Smoking my fag away
Cough, cough, cough, cough
I was kicked out by a guard
Cough, cough, cough, cough
And landed hard
Cough, cough, cough, cough

I was in the hospital one day
Seeing my life pass away
Cough, cough, cough, cough
It's not a joke
You shouldn't smoke!
Cough, cough, cough, cough
Cough, cough, cough, cough

...Eat me!

GET A LIFE!

SMOKING IS DANGEROUS
It's like eating an anaconda
It's like sitting on a crocodile
SMOKING IS DANGEROUS
NEVER TRY IT AT ALL
It's like eating a firework
It's like playing with a chainsaw
SMOKING IS DANGEROUS
NEVER TRY IT AT ALL
It's like drinking a canal
It's like biting a shark
SMOKING IS DANGEROUS
NEVER TRY IT AT ALL

NEVER, NEVER, TRY THESE THINGS AT ALL
DON'T SMOKE, GET A LIFE!

Beckie Spooner

BIN 'EM!

A cigarette is a straw in a glass of tar
waiting to be drunk;
A cigarette is a puddle of acid rain
dripping down your throat;
A cigarette is a poison pen
leaking into your lungs;
A cigarette is a dye
putting stains on your fingers and teeth.

Bin 'em!

Leigh Jones

VOLCANO

You think you're harder than Vinnie Jones
But your clothes smell.
You think you're trendy and sexy
But you're on the road to sacrifice.
You think you're relaxed
But there's a volcano erupting in your stomach.

Paul Yeomans

DO YOU STILL
WANT TO TRY IT?

Some people think it's cool to smoke
Don't be daft, don't even joke
Once you start, it's hard to pack it in
Like other drugs, it becomes an addiction
Tobacco takes its toll on your health
The price it costs leaves a hole in your wealth
Nicotine is a deadly habit
See a ciggie, gotta grab it
The magazines make it look so cool
But don't forget the golden rule
Smoking often causes cancer
Do you feel lucky, are you a chancer?
It makes you ill or even worse
So just take a minute to read this verse

Do you still want to try it?

Natalie Simms

HIGGLEDY, PIGGLEDY, COUGHEDY, COUGH

Don't smoke, don't smoke
or you will choke.
It won't make you tough.
It won't make you rough.
In the end you will have had enough
but you've already smoked too much.
      You'll probably die!!

Think of what you'll be like -
bad breath, greasy hair,
yellow teeth, finger and toes and
perhaps even your cute little nose.
Higgledy, piggledy, coughedy, cough,
what a noisy cough you've got.
Hu, pu, what a terrible smell and it's all
coming from you.

But wait, that's not all -
you might get cancer,
and much, much more . . .
I hope you'll understand why I'm
saying all this.
You'll probably say that I'm a pain.
well that's a shame because I'll say it
again and again.

Don't smoke, don't smoke
or you will choke.
It won't make you tough.
It won't make you rough.
In the end you will have had enough
but you've already smoked too much.
      You'll probably die!!

Michelle Cartwright

THE FOREST OF ARDEN

Smoke chokes the big trees
They may be ill and die.
The trees haven't got enough air
in the smoking forest of Arden.

The saw cuts down the big trees.
The tree doesn't like it
it's scared.
The fruit would fall down to the
ground
in the smoking forest of Arden.

A smoking tree with crispy leaves of
brown,
The little branches will fall off
in the smoking forest of Arden.

Primary 2
Arden School.

SMOKING KILLS!

Smoking kills
Puts up the bills
Your lifespan shrinks
Your breath stinks
Your fingers go yellow
You think you're so mellow
Your lungs will go pop
And your heart will stop

Remember - smoking kills!

Laura Viney

AN ARMY IS COMING AT ME

An army is coming at me,
All because I smoke.

An army is coming at me,
And it is making me choke.

An army is coming at me,
Straight through my mouth.

An army is coming at me,
And it is heading deep down south.

An army is coming at me,
And it is clogging up my blood.

An army is coming at me,
I know I should stop, if only I could.

An army is coming at me,
I have got to fight back.

An army is coming at me,
And smoking has got the sack.

Benjamin Charles & Benjamin Butler

A CIGARETTE IS . . .

A cigarette is a rubber,
  erasing away your lungs
A cigarette is a gun,
  firing at your unborn baby
A cigarette is old perfume,
  making your clothes smell
A cigarette is a dye,
  colouring your lungs black

Hayley Rowlands

THE SILLY YOUNG MAN FROM WEST BROM.

My friend likes fags
He started smoking at 10
and could not stop.

At the age of 12
He was mad over them.
I said to him "You've got to stop."
But he carried on smoking
Throughout the years.

When he was 30
He said "This wouldn't even kill a bus."
So he carried on smoking.

When he was 60
He had a bad case of heart disease
No-one would marry him
'Cause of the smoke wafting around his
house.

When he was 70
He died of bad cancer
Because of the smoke
The silly young man from West Brom.

Lee Thompson

TERANCE THE TRAIN

Terance the train puffs out smoke
Terance the train gives you heart disease
Terance the train makes you choke
Terance the train gives you heart disease

Terance the train gives you asthma
Terance the train gives you heart disease
Terance the train gives you a cough
Terance the train gives you heart disease

Terance the train crashes into a wall.

David Plimmer

SUCH A GOOD IDEA?

Cigarettes are dangerous,
As dangerous as:
> jumping in petrol
> playing with matches
> playing with gas
> jumping into a fire
> going close to an unexploded bomb

Cigarettes are dangerous,
As dangerous as:
> an earthquake
> putting matches in your eyes
> nasty places
> people with bombs
> witches on the streets

Smoking is a bad idea for children and adults
You could get cancer
You could die of cancer
Now do you think smoking is such a good idea?

Rubi Akhtar

CHEERFUL, THE CHIMNEY SMOKER

Cheerful, the chimney smoker,
loves to play poker.
He's my best friend but
he drives me round the bend.
People think he's hot
but really he's not.

He's a pain.

Chloe Quinn

AS SMELLY AS . . .

As smelly as smelly socks,
  sweat dripping off my forehead,
  people smoking in a pub.

As smelly as dog muck on the bottom of my shoe,
  tyres burning in a skip,
  smoking five cigarettes in an hour.

As smelly as a dustbin lorry going past my house
  a dustbin falling over, right outside my door,
  smoke going up my nose.

Lee Taylor & Richard Brookes

BURNING UP YOUR IMAGE

You think it relaxes you, like a Jacuzzi
but really it's leaving trails of ash where your lungs used to be.
You think it makes you look cool like Will Smith
but really it's burning up your image.
You smoke because you think
you're going to look smart
and you think
you'll be part of the gang
but really you stink
so no-one wants to go near you.
You think that it's not going to harm you
but really it's like a knife
stabbing you in your heart,
every time you smoke.

Nicola Beddington

GIVE UP NOW

A cigarette is a factory chimney
polluting everything around it.
Give up now, or you'll regret it.

A cigarette is a casino,
making you gamble with your life.
Give up now, or you'll regret it.

A cigarette is a king,
making you follow him.
Give up now, or you'll regret it.

A cigarette is an army,
driving tanks all over your lungs.
Give up now, or you'll regret it.

A cigarette is a train,
puffing its way to the final stop.
Give up now, or you'll regret it.

Rebecca Price

INCY WINCY SPIDER

Incy Wincy Spider had a fag in his gob

Incy Wincy Spider climbed the smoky spout
Then down came the rain and washed the fag out

But Incy Wincy Spider was never seen again

Lee Pryce

JACK AND JILL

Jack and Jill went up the hill to have a couple of fags.
They had a smoke but Jack did choke, and so did Jill soon after.

Harriet Emerson & Samantha Warwick

BEFORE

Tobacco is a plant
it contains nicotine
it contains tar
it depresses the appetite
yet it is legal

Tobacco raises money through taxes
it is expensive
it is a stimulant
it is addictive
yet it is legal

Tobacco comes from America
it is a legal drug
it killed my grandma

Yet it smells nice before you smoke it

Margaret Peach

YES .... BUT

Yes tobacco is legal
But it killed my nan
Yes tobacco is addictive
And you must stop if you can.

Yes tobacco contains tar
(I thought you get that on the roads)
Yes tobacco is expensive
I will stop if I can!

Yes tobacco causes cancer
And heart diseases too
Yes it can make your breath stink
But can I stop? Yes ..... I think!

Teresa Kelly & Anna Cannings

WORSE

A cigarette is like a pair of scissors - cutting your life short.
What else is a cigarette like?
A cigarette is like a long thin rope - around your neck.
What else is a cigarette like?
A cigarette is like a ticking bomb - waiting to explode.
What else is a cigarette like?
A cigarette is like a blazing fire - burning inside your lungs.
What else is a cigarette like?
A cigarette is like a great wizard - making your money disappear.
What else is a cigarette like?
A cigarette is like a black hole - sucking you into an addiction.

A pair of scissors,
a long thin rope,
a ticking bomb,
a blazing fire,
a great wizard,
a black hole,
a cigarette.

But out of all these, the cigarette is definitely worse.

Hayley John

TAR FREE ZONES

Without you, my lungs would be tar free zones,
Without you I would have big, healthy bones.
Without you, my breath would have a nice scent,
Without you, it'll be like an angel that's been sent.
Without you, my life would be free,
Without you, I will be me.

Ian Farnell

SIGNS OF LIFE

NO SMOKING in the taxi
NO SMOKING in the church
NO SMOKING in the bakery
NO SMOKING at your work

NO SMOKING in the chip shop
NO SMOKING at the vets
NO SMOKING signs are everywhere
Say no to cigarettes!

Victoria Swanson

IF CIGARETTES WERE . . .

If cigarettes were rock
            they'd break your bones
            make you bleed
            bruise your body
            make your fingernails go black
If cigarettes were rock.

 If cigarettes were acid
            they would burn you
            fry you
            scorch you
If cigarettes were acid.

If cigarettes were 'Sir'
            they would make you write lines
            make you read stories off the OHP
            deafen you
            make you stay in at dinnertime
If cigarettes were 'Sir'.

But there's a smokescreen and we can't
see the harm inside.

Chris Madeley

I KNEW A BOY . .
I KNEW A GIRL

I knew a boy who found some money
He bought some fags and felt really funny
In the end he had black lungs
And a really nasty tongue
His teeth are now luminous yella
(He's a very uncool fella)
He always wanted to be a dancer
He can't now 'cos he's got cancer
  To him a cigarette's a murderer

I knew a girl called Joanne Threith
Who mysteriously had green teeth
No-one knew why they were so green
Everyone thought she was very unclean
In fact she brushed them every day
A cigarette just doesn't pay
People don't want to know her anymore
She threw her fags onto the floor
She doesn't want to see them any more
  To her a cigarette's a murderer

Laura Mason

DON'T EVEN THINK ABOUT IT!

Don't even think about trying to smoke!
Only people that don't smoke have a better chance to live longer.
No Smoking signs are up, so read them and do it!
To smoke you need money, which you could spend on your family.

Some people don't live because of smoking.
More and more places such as factories, shopping centres, are 'no smoking' places.
Operations have to be done, and some may fail!
King size cigarettes are the worst!!
Even if there is someone in your family that smokes, you could die breathing in their
  smoke - this is called passive smoking!!!

Hayley Noke

TICK, TOCK

Smoking is cool
now I'm growing up
Tick, tock, Tick, tock
Me and my friends
think it's fun
Tick, tock
I'm a bully
holding my cigarette
looking bored
Tick, tock, Tick, tock
I smoke 60 a day
Tick, tock
It's burning me away
Tick, tock, Tick, tock
Burning inside
I'm going to die
Tick . . . .

Samantha Duffy

A BREATH OF FRESH AIR

My Dad used to smoke,
All we did was choke, choke, choke.
The walls were brown -
It made us frown -
They looked like a filter, nicotine brown.
One day my Dad got up,
Decided he'd had enough.
At first he was sad,
He felt so, so bad.

A few weeks later, he began to smile,
It was surely worth his while.
And now he's given smoking up,
The walls are white,
The choking has stopped
And everything smells much sweeter.

Read my poem,
Remember what I've wrote -
Don't make yourself or others choke.

Jessica Adams

AS NAUGHTY AS . . .

As naughty as
Poking people
Cheeking my teacher
Back-chatting my parents
Tricking people
Trying your first cigarette
As naughty as

As naughty as
Fighting in school
Swearing at people
Getting hooked on nicotine
Smoking after school
As naughty as

Katie Owen & Terrie Dicken

BECAUSE . . .

A cigarette is like a chimney
puffing deadly smoke out.
So why do I smoke?

Smoking is like a bomb
ticking inside my lungs.
So why do I smoke?

Cigarettes are like fire balls
wrapping around my lungs,
stopping me from breathing.
So why do I smoke?

Because . . . it's addictive.

Laura White

FAG ASH LIL

Meet my girlfriend Lil, Fag Ash for short,
For here are a few lessons that need to be taught.
Many people know Fag Ash and, with common knowledge,
Many people know that she graduated from college.
She threw her knowledge away
By not listening to what people say.
Fag Ash could harm you within a day.
She takes my hand and leads me astray.
What can I say? Really, I don't want to stay.
She's urging me to smoke,
She just thinks it's a joke.
She wants to stop my heart from beating,
Catch a disease such as cancer,
So then I will never be a dancer.
She wants to fill my lungs with thick black tar.
I don't think so, ha, ha, ha.
My lovely golden hair would be dull and miserable
But she wouldn't care.
My teeth would be yellow with dirty horrible brown stains
And that would be a real pain.
She wants my clothes to smell of nicotine,
So everyone will know just where I've been.
She wants my finger nails to turn yellow
And expects me to be like her - a horrible fellow.
She says smoking won't stop my growth
But I know from research, it will harm us both.
She says "Just take one drag of this fag,
then another and then maybe another,
I'll never tell your mother".
She makes me feel so uneasy.
I say NO! - I want to feel bright and breezy,
Not coughing, choking and wheezy.
I don't need a bad friend like Fag Ash,
I'll save my cash.
I will listen to sensible advice
And hope other people will too.
So flush out the fags
And throw them down the loo.
Stay healthy, think healthy, be healthy.
Don't die for a fag!

Hayley Stokes

SMOKESCREEN

If cigarettes were rollers, they would
squash you
pop your eyes out
flatten you
break your bones.
If cigarettes were rollers.

If cigarettes were sharks, they would
eat you
rip your arms off
rip you into shreds
rip your flesh.
If cigarettes were sharks.

If cigarettes were bombs, they would
blow you off your feet
make your blood splat everywhere
make your hair spike up.
If cigarettes were bombs.

If cigarettes were hammers, they would
give you a lump on your head
crack your head open
make you dizzy
give you a bruise.
If cigarettes were hammers.

But there's a smokescreen and we can't
see the harm inside.

Sean Young

THE KING OF SMOKE

The King of Smoke will take over
The King of Smoke will kill you
The King of Smoke will take your taxes

The King of Smoke has a deep, speechless voice
The King of Smoke has discoloured teeth
The King of Smoke smells
The King of Smoke has asthma
The King of Smoke has lung cancer
The King of Smoke has heart disease
The King of Smoke can kill at any time
The King of Smoke is made of smoke

Don't let the King of Smoke take over!

Kirandeep Kaur

WHAT ELSE COULD
A CIGARETTE BE?

A cigarette is like a chimney, puffing all day.
A cigarette is like a poacher, stalking its prey.

What else could a cigarette be?

A cigarette is like a dark room, without any light.
A cigarette is like a dagger, slashing at your life.

What else could a cigarette be?

A cigarette is like a pet, your best buddy.
A cigarette is like a thief, stealing your money.

What else could a cigarette be?

Adele Johnson

CIGARETTES CAN KILL

Cigarettes can kill,
smoke in your lungs will make you ill.
Go to the chemist for a nicotine patch
around £3.99, it's not much cash
each for the packet and you will see
extra cash for you and me.
Take my advice and you won't need
to smoke that nasty weed.
Everything you need to know -
stop smoking and you will grow.

Richard Campbell

FAGS ARE AN ARMY

FAGS ARE DANGEROUS
They make you smell
FAGS CAUSE ADDICTION
We can tell
FAGS ARE LIKE A DAGGER
Piercing your heart
IF YOU HAVEN'T TRIED THEM YET
Then just don't start
FAGS MAKE YOU COUGH
Splutter and choke
THAT'S WHY YOU SHOULD NEVER, EVER
SMOKE

Fags are dangerous
THEY SPOIL YOUR HEALTH
Fags cause cancer
AND STEAL YOUR WEALTH
Fags cause heart disease
AND BLOCK THE VEINS
Discolour your fingers
AND DAMAGE THE BRAIN

**Ria Kinsella, Rachel Roberts, David Bone,
Drew Canavan, Paul Bird & Stephen Cunningham**

DO YOU FEEL LUCKY?

Cigarettes all contain tobacco
Friends chant "Give it a go"
Just one puff is all it takes
To get you addicted to those flakes.

Strike a match, alight at last
This is easy, what a blast!
Smoking's a habit you can't break
It's like a drug you have to take.

Cigars and pipes are just as bad
The effects are forever, not just a fad
Smoking causes cancer which can kill
So if you start, better make a will!

Do you feel lucky?

Jessica Simms

A DAGGER

A cigarette is like a chimney
        because it blows smoke in your face
A cigarette is like a bin
        because it contains a lot of rubbish
A cigarette is like a crayon
        because it colours your fingers

And most of all

A cigarette is like a dagger
        choking you in your throat

Shereen Thompson

TORNADO & VOLCANO

My cigarette is a tornado
    leaving scraps behind;
My cigarette is a fire
    harming the forest;
My cigarette is a fizzy drink
    colouring my teeth;
My cigarette is perfume
    leaving a smell behind;
My cigarette is gold
    too expensive to buy;
My cigarette is a firework
    wonderful but dangerous;
My cigarette is a gun
    shooting at my heart;
My cigarette is ink
    colouring my lungs;
My cigarette is a chimney
    leaving smoke behind;
My cigarette is a volcano
    bursting out with lava.

Harpreet Gill

AS NASTY AS . . .

As nasty as . . .
    Filling your lungs with tar,
    Swimming in a pool of ashes,
    Taking drugs.

As nasty as . . .
    Dying for a couple of minutes of enjoyment,
    Burning your lips,
    Having yellow hands and teeth.

As nasty as . . .
    Eating a bowl of ashes,
    Sucking on tar,
    Coughing your life away.

Wesley Revell

TOM, TOM, THE PIPER'S SON

Tom, Tom, the Piper's son
stole a fag and away did run.
He can't run fast,
he can't run quick,
all that smoke has made him sick.
He ran to his mom,
who was rather mad.
She said "Dear Tom,
you're a very bad lad.
All that smoking will choke your lungs.
You'll never play the pipe for your mates and chums.
I know your throat is very sore.
So I'd advise you, Tom, to smoke no more."

Jennie Senior & Natasha Jones

STOP SMOKING

Smoking is bad for your health
Think of the damage you do
Our bodies don't want us to smoke
Passive smoking can harm you too

So think about stopping the fags
Make a big effort today
Our bodies are special to us
Keep them healthy if you care
It's up to you to make it work
No-one thinks it's cool
Go on and stop smoking today

Harprem Jagpal

MY LUNGS

My lungs are as free as air
My lungs are as free as a butterfly's wings
My lungs are as free as birds singing in the sky
My lungs are as free as bees buzzing
My lungs are as free as wasps flying
My lungs are as free as balloons floating
My lungs are as free as leaves whirling in the breeze

Keep my lungs free,
Don't smoke around me

Class IG (Mixed Y1/2)
Old Park Primary School

NO SMOKING

No, I don't want to breathe in your smoke
Open the window before I choke

Smoking is bad for your health
Makes you smell and stains your fingers
Once you start, you cannot stop
Kick the habit or you will drop
It isn't big and it isn't smart
Never begin, never start
Give it up, it's bad for your heart

Natalie Baugh

I HOPE NOT

Nicotine taking over like a monster
Leaving its life-long stain
Gasping for breath yet again
Puffing, wheezing, coughing
Wanting another fag
Lungs turning black as night
Cancer spreading round the body
Stinking breath
Trying to hide away the yellow marks
on fingers and teeth.
Addicted for life?
I hope not!

Amy Webb, Jenny Fullwood & Tia Rageh

MY CIGARETTE IS . . .

My cigarette is a chimney blackening my lungs
My cigarette is a scaffold holding up my temptation
My cigarette is a knife cutting my life away
My cigarette is a grenade setting off to kill me
My cigarette is a hole-punch punching me to death
My cigarette is a key opening the door of death.

Andrew Fisher

THE MOUSE TRAP

A cigarette is like
cheese in a mouse trap, luring you towards death,
an old woman shrinking away.
What else can a cigarette be?

A cigarette is like
a detention - taking time away from you,
a heart - irreplaceable when it's worn out.
What else can a cigarette be?

A cigarette is like
a day here - just a waste of time.
What else can a cigarette be?

Natasha Watson

DO YOU THINK . . . ?

Do you think it's ace to smoke?
Acting like a cool dude
Spending all your cash
Smelling like some ash.

Do you think it's cool to smoke?
Acting like a joker
Out of breath playing football
Not growing very tall.

So you think it's big to smoke?
Acting like a clown
While you're puffing away
Your body suffers every day.

Daniel Deen

DAY BY DAY

A dagger, stabbing my heart.
A nuclear warhead
leaving ash on my lungs.
A stink bomb
leaving a smell
on my hands and clothes.
Gateway to death.
Turning my body into ash,
day by day,
month by month,
year by year,
puff by puff.

James Bonness

IN MEMORY OF THE WORLD'S WORST SMOKER

Guess what I like?
It is smoke.
Suddenly one day,
My lungs nearly broke.

I had to go to hospital
Because of the pain.
A few days later,
It started again.

The doctor gave me pills
But they didn't work.
A day later,
My lungs gave a jerk.

I went to the doctors,
They checked in my head.
A few days later,
I was dead!!

Andrew Wilson, Paul Aherne, Craig Martin &
Karim Hmaissi

DAVID THE DRAGON

David the Dragon tries to kill you
He stops you running
He is keen and cunning
David the Dragon makes your hair turn grey
He knows you will need a fag every day
David the Dragon makes you look old
David the Dragon is very, very bold.

Charlotte Parkes

SMOKING IS DANGEROUS

Smoking is dangerous:
It's like drinking poison
or chewing a snake.
It's like being pushed
into a burning building
or eating out of the dustbin.
It's like chewing an old boot
or smelling toxic waste
or putting a rope
around your neck
and pulling it tight.

Stop smoking.
Get fit.

Matthew Caville

FIGHT THE WAR

Cigarettes are like revolutionaries
                IGNORE THE PROPAGANDA
Trying to destroy the fabric of your health,
small bands armed to the teeth attack
the outposts of your body
                IGNORE THE PROPAGANDA
Breaking down your resistance, ready to make
the final assault on the HEART AND LUNGS
the capital of your body
                IGNORE THE PROPAGANDA

Like a revolution it could take many years
to break you down with battles along the way,
a stroke, a heart attack, maybe an amputated limb
                HEED THE WARNINGS
The closer they get to the capital
the more serious it becomes
                HEED THE WARNINGS
Communication like your circulation and
respiration becomes more restricted
                HEED THE WARNINGS

As they lay siege to your vital organs
you wish you had ignored the propaganda
and heeded the warnings
But it's too late as they finally break down
the city walls and overrun the capital
and take control despatching you to
                YOUR GRAVE

J.S. Bishton

THE SILLY OLD BLOKE

I once knew a bloke
He used to smoke
His health was bad
Everyone thought he was sad.

I once knew a bloke
He used to smoke
He lost his hair
But he didn't care.

I once knew a bloke
He used to smoke
His lungs were black
As black as his mack.

I once knew a bloke
He used to smoke
His breath smelt stale
Then he went pale
He started to choke
     and that was
          the end of
             the
               silly
             old
               bloke.

Samantha Shenston

AS STUPID AS . . .

As stupid as . . .
>
> Not listening to your doctor
>
> Smashing your window
>
> Injecting yourself with drugs
>
> Inhaling nicotine from cigarette smoke

As stupid as . . .
>
> Sniffing glue
>
> Threatening to kill someone if they don't do as you say
>
> Walking on glass
>
> Making someone else smoke

As stupid as . . .
>
> Committing suicide
>
> Doing graffiti
>
> Blackmailing for a stupid reason
>
> Trying to buy cigarettes under age

They make smoking sound cool
>
> but is killing yourself really cool?

Beth Haylings & Rebekah Roper

PREPARE FOR ACTION

Smoking brings an army

Armies can kill

They lay barbed wire in your mouth

PREPARE FOR ACTION!
PREPARE FOR ACTION!

They light gunpowder in your throat

PREPARE FOR ACTION!
PREPARE FOR ACTION!

They put dynamite in your chest

PREPARE FOR ACTION!
PREPARE FOR ACTION!

They shoot rockets at your lungs

PREPARE FOR ACTION!
PREPARE FOR ACTION!

They plant mines in your heart

PREPARE FOR ACTION
AND FIGHT BACK!!

Luke Finnegan & Sean Madden

SMOKING RUINS

strip the cellophane
pull the pin on another packet

lob
          a ballistic arc
to the lips
              like a grenadier

it's an anti-personnel mine/yours/theirs
it doesn't care
               who it gets
           it has no conscience

foundations shake with each impact

the chest recoils
as
snipers cough from windows
in the smoking ruins
of a body
               under siege

Dave Reeves

Rachael Doody